Nelson Grammar

Denis and Helen Ballance

Book 2

Nelson

Contents

Do you remember?	4, 5
Simple sentences	6
Expanding simple sentences	7
Compound sentences	8
Conjunctions	9
Negatives	10
Sentences: word order	11
Revision	12
Just for fun	13
Different kinds of nouns	14
Proper and common nouns	15
Personal titles	16
Dictionary order by second letters	17
Pronouns	18
Special pronouns	19
Plurals: words ending in **ch** and **sh**	20
Plurals: words ending in **ay**, **ey**, **oy**, **uy**	21
Revision	22
Just for fun	23
Adjectives	24
Possessive adjectives	25
Verbs: tense	26
Present continuous tense	27
Different forms of the past tense	28
Past participles	29
Subject and verb agreement	30
Punctuation at the end of a sentence	31
Commas	32
Apostrophes in short forms	33
Revision	34
Just for fun	35
Paragraphs	36
Paragraphs in stories	37
Adjectives: countries	38
Confusing words: their, there	39
Short forms of words	40
Short forms: initials	41
Unusual plurals	42
Plurals: words ending in **f** and **fe**	43
Three common mistakes	44
Names and addresses	45
Revision	46
Just for fun	47
Index	48

Introduction

Grammar is the name given to the rules for writing and speaking English. Because English is spoken in so many parts of the world, it is important that everyone who uses it should keep to the same rules.

Nelson Grammar is a series of books which sets out to explain some of the rules of grammar. The rules given in this book have been chosen because they are the ones you need to know at this stage of your school life. As well as rules dealing with such things as capital letters, punctuation and word order, the books introduce and explain some of the special words used in grammar.

Nelson Grammar is designed to be used alongside your other work in language. Each page spotlights a single grammar topic and is intended to provide the central point for one week's work.

Read the rules and examples given in the green patch at the top of each page first. After you have studied the rules carefully, do the exercises which provide practice in applying them. Here and there, you will find 'Just for fun' and Revision pages.

At the end of the book, there is an index to help you to look up topics you may need when you are writing. Please do not write the answers to the puzzles and exercises in this book.

Do you remember?

Write these sentences, choosing the correct word from the brackets.
1. 'lemon' comes (before   after) 'orange' in the dictionary.
2. Sentences begin with (small   capital) letters.
3. The fifth letter in the alphabet is (d   e   f)
4. This path leads (to   too   two) Westgate.
5. He is the leader (of   off) the gang.
6. The plural of 'hiss' is ('hisses'   'hisss')
7. A short form of 'do not' is ('do'nt'   'don't')

8. He gave me (a   an) empty glass.
9. 'Pig' is a (singular   plural) noun.
10. Paula lives in (margate   Margate).
11. This is (a   an) good breakfast.
12. John fell (of   off) the branch.
13. My birthday is on (june   June) 1st.
14. They (are   were) both ill last week.
15. Her name is (Pat York   pat york)
16. We (was   were) late for dinner.
17. John is captain (of   off) the team.

18. There are (to   too   two) nests in this hedge.
19. The singular of 'follies' is ('folly'   'follie')
20. 'heavy' is a (noun   verb   adjective)
21. 'bedroom' is a (collective   compound) noun.
22. 'pack' is a (collective   compound) noun.
23. They came on (Easter Sunday   easter sunday)
24. ('butter'   'tea') comes after 'cheese' in the dictionary.
25. My grandfather was (to   too   two) ill to go to the birthday party.
26. What happened last year is called the (past   present   future)
27. The allied armies were commanded by (field marshal robins   Field Marshal Robins)

Do you remember?

A Read these sentences and answer the questions in the boxes below.

1 Have you ever seen a stoat?
2 It is a small animal with a chestnut coat and a black tip to its short tail.
3 A pack of stoats will attack dogs and even their owners.
4 They hunt rabbits, rats and mice.
5 In Scotland and Northern England, stoats turn white in winter but the tips of their tails remain black.

Sentence 1
A How is this sentence different from all the others?
B What is the mark at the end of it called?

Sentence 2
A Write the four nouns in this sentence.
B Find the four adjectives that describe the nouns.

Sentence 3
A What is the verb in this sentence?
B Find a collective noun.

Sentence 4
A What is the verb?
B The three nouns are all plurals. Write their singulars.

Sentence 5
A This is a long sentence in two parts. Which is the joining word between its two parts?
B Which noun does the adjective 'black' describe?
C Which noun does the adjective 'white' describe?
D Why do 'Scotland' and 'Northern England' begin with capital letters?

B Write the plurals of these words.

fox   tooth   child   trellis   boss   duty   ceremony   ally   woman

Simple sentences

Here is a simple sentence. **Simon kicked the ball.**

It falls into two parts.

The subject: **Simon**   The predicate: **kicked the ball**

The subject is the main person or thing written about.

The predicate includes the verb. It also includes the object where there is one. It completes what is happening in the sentence.

A Divide these sentences into subjects and predicates. Underline the verbs.

1. Lions roam the grasslands.
2. The pony and the mule ran away.
3. The cat scratched David's face.
4. Cowboys attacked the Indians.
5. Ann found Jo's dog in the road.
6. A bus hit their car.

B Join these subjects and predicates to make simple sentences.

1 The dog	make bread.	4 Comedians	build nests.
2 Wind	ate a bone.	5 Frost	entertain us.
3 Bakers	dries washing.	6 Birds	bursts water pipes.

Join the subjects in the green boxes with predicates from the black boxes to make sensible sentences.

A policeman — caught a cold — The bowler — caught a mouse

caught the ball — caught a fish — Mr Perkins — The angler

caught the thief — The cat — caught a bus — Miss Ray

Expanding simple sentences

We can add adjectives or extra nouns to the subject and object to make the sentence more interesting.

The adjectives and extra nouns are counted as parts of the subject and object.

Simon kicked the ball.
↓
Young Simon kicked the heavy ball.

subject	verb	object
Young Simon	kicked	the heavy ball.

A Write these sentences. Divide them into subject, verb and object.

1. A nasty man kicked my new bicycle.
2. A savage dog bit my little sister.
3. Two strong men carried a heavy box.
4. Their brother won the annual race.
5. A massive yellow bulldozer destroyed the beautiful old house.

B Write the subject of each of these sentences. Each one has two nouns.

1. Rex and Judy crossed the bridge.
2. The man at the desk gives the orders.
3. A shoal of fish broke our nets.
4. Mary's brother opened the box.
5. The leader of the outlaw band threw me into the dark cellar.

Arrange the green words into four different sentences to describe what is happening in each of the four pictures.

umbrella   short
man   an   The
hit   with   the
tall   lady

7

Compound sentences

Two simple sentences may be joined by **and** or **but** to make a compound sentence.

and usually shows that the second sentence follows on naturally from the first.

but usually shows that the second sentence says something unexpected or surprising.

Examples: The rain stopped **and** we felt much happier.

The rain stopped **but** we were no better off.

A Join these sentences together with and

1. My head aches. I feel dizzy.
2. The savage tiger escaped from its cage. All the people ran away.
3. No rain has fallen for three months. The farmers' crops are dying.
4. The back leg of the chair broke. Tom fell heavily to the floor.

B Use and or but to join these sentences.

1. Six of their players were injured. They won the match easily.
2. Garry twisted his ankle in the park. He walked home unaided.
3. Helen's green skirt is in the wash. Her brown one needs mending.
4. The airliner crashed moments after take-off. No-one was injured.

Make compound sentences by writing simple sentences about each of these pairs of pictures and then joining them together.

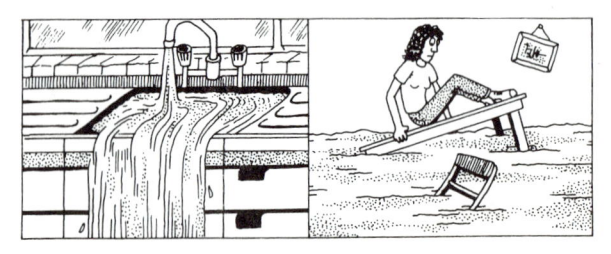

Conjunctions

and and **but** are called conjunctions. They are used to join two sentences of equal importance. If one sentence is more important than the other, different conjunctions may be used. Then the conjunction can completely alter the meaning.

Example:

He left **before** it had ended.

He left **after** it had ended.

The meanings of these two sentences are quite different although only the conjunction has been changed.

A Find the conjunction in each of these sentences. Write the number of the sentence and its conjunction.

1. Donkeys bray but horses neigh.
2. We rested while Janet went on.
3. They waited until Tim had gone.
4. I sing because I am happy.
5. I carried on although I was tired.
6. Dogs may bite if you tease them.

B Write these sentences. Choose conjunctions from the box to fill the spaces.

| and   although   unless   because   until |

1. He lit the fire ——— the children were very cold.
2. You will not be allowed into the ground ——— you have a ticket.
3. The lions were not fed ——— just before the visitors arrived.
4. The dog got out of its basket ——— followed them into the kitchen.
5. He tried to reach the fort ——— he was suffering from frost bite.

Make as many sentences as you can by putting different conjunctions in the space.

The army marched away from Moscow ——— the winter weather closed in.

Negatives

not and **no** are very important words.

By adding **not** or **no** it is possible to change the meaning of a sentence completely.

Example: I am afraid of snakes.

I am not afraid of snakes.

Take care when you use two negatives in one sentence.

Example:

He is no longer one of those who does not smoke.

It really means, 'He now smokes'.

A Add not or no to each sentence to make it mean the exact opposite.

1. This is a straight line.
2. There is sense in what he says.
3. These animals are dangerous.
4. Camping is allowed in this park.
5. The new sums are difficult.
6. Trains use this line on Sundays.

B These are short forms of negative phrases. Write them in full.

don't   can't   isn't   wouldn't   daren't   doesn't   won't   didn't   shan't

C Write the meaning of the following sentences in the smallest number of words you can.

1. It is not true that the dog is not dangerous.
2. No-one wanted not to go.
3. Soldiers are not allowed not to attend church.

Write a word from the box to match each picture.

non-stop
non-smoker
non-fiction

10

Sentences: word order

The order of words in a sentence may be changed for certain reasons.

1 To write the same thing in a different way.

   Example:

   It is now summer in Australia.

   In Australia, it is now summer.

2 To change the meaning.

   Example:

   The cowboys chased the Indians.

   The Indians chased the cowboys.

A Change the word order in these sentences but keep the same meaning.
1 The swallows fly away to the south before winter comes.
2 After the burglar had gone, Mrs Johnson called the police.
3 You see the same people in the market every day.
4 Cannibals lived on this island in the days of Captain Cook.

B Give these sentences exactly opposite meanings by writing their words in a different order.
1 Peter Morris hit Brian Green.
2 A car ran into the back of a bus.
3 A chair fell on Mary.
4 They drove from Bath to Bristol.
5 The bear ate Mr Swift.
6 Miss Smith arrived before Tim.

Use these words to write six sentences with different meanings.

first   saw
the   lions
the   men

11

Revision

> The subject is what the sentence is about.

> A compound sentence is two or more simple sentences joined by a conjunction such as **and** or **but**

> The verb is the 'doing' or action word.

A Answer these five questions for each of the sentences numbered 1 to 5 below.

A   Is this a simple or a compound sentence?   B   Which word (or words) makes up the verb?   C   Does the sentence ask a question?   D   Which word is the subject?   E   Is the action taking place in the past, the present or the future?

Example:

Bears overturned the dustbins.

A simple   B overturned
C no   D bears   E past

---

1. Alison will deliver the parcel.
2. Peanuts will grow on the stems.
3. Paul scrubbed the table and washed the dishes.
4. Don was a good swimmer but he was not the best.
5. May Sue go out now?

B Find five conjunctions in these sentences.

Iceland is in the far north but in summer the days are long. The sun rises early and sets late. Plants grow quickly because the soil is warm. Flowers bloom overnight since they must set seeds before the long winter returns.

C Add **no** or **not** to give these sentences opposite meanings.

1. This is a public footpath.
2. There are cows in the field.
3. Guests are expected to pay.
4. Oranges grow in Scotland.
5. Do take your work home.
6. The dog is very obedient.

Just for fun

A A picture has been stolen from its frame. Find out what the picture is about by reading the words in the green grid below. The black grid tells you the correct word order. Read word number 1, then word number 2 and so on. The first two words are 'This is . . .'

25	21	9	8	12
24	22	1	2	7
20	17	14	10	6
23	16	4	13	19
15	5	3	18	11

home.	the	some	where	It
gone	cows	This	is	field
all	foggy	a	cows	a
have	cold	picture	is	and
very	of	a	day	live.

B Here are some descriptions of birds. Can you guess what they are? The letters on their eggs, put in order, spell out their names.

This bird is small and brown. It has red feathers on its breast. Its nest is built in old walls, old saucepans or in any convenient hole.

This bird has a hooked beak and sharp talons. Its feathers are chestnut brown and grey. It lives on mice and beetles.

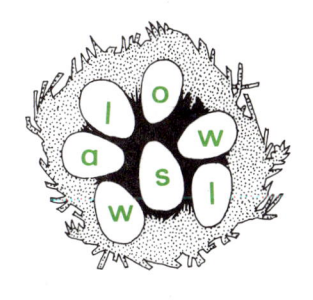

This bird has a blue back and wings. The lower parts are brown and white. It has a forked tail. Its nest is made of mud and grass. It lives on insects.

Different kinds of nouns

A noun is a name word.

Some nouns are names of things you can see and touch.

Examples:

book   chair   orange   flowers

Other nouns are names of qualities, feelings and other things you cannot see.

Examples:

fear   bravery   peace   escape

roar   whisper   end   beginning

A Write the two nouns in each of these sentences. One is the name of something you can see; the other is the name of something you cannot.

1   The final loud snore awoke my aunt.

2   Both islands are famous for their beauty.

3   The dark forest is full of unknown dangers.

4   They were sitting in the middle of the river.

B Write sentences containing these nouns.

1 mystery   2 happiness   3 care   4 memory   5 speed

C Find ten nouns in these sentences.

Donna jumped up from the chair. A jabbing pain shot through her arm. An insect had bitten her. Could it be a mosquito? Their high-pitched buzzing had disturbed the peace of the riverside all afternoon.

dream   spade   idea   sleep
nothing   uproar   pillow
walnut   offer   melon
advice   book   rumble

Pick out the eight green nouns that are names of things you cannot see. Put their first letters together and re-arrange them to make the name of the animal that made the footprint.

Proper and common nouns

When a noun is the name of a particular thing or place, it begins with a capital letter and is called a proper noun.

Examples: Bristol   Gaumont   City Rd   Granada   January

A noun that is the name of a thing of which there are many different examples begins with a small letter and is called a common noun.

Examples: city   car   cinema   aeroplane   sailor   book   bed

A Write the eight proper nouns in this list. Make their first letters capitals.

mars   carpet   coventry   july   horse   drain   snowdon   denmark   crocus   concorde   floor   lemon   vauxhall   teapot   thursday

B The main words in the names of books, plays, television programmes and buildings begin with capital letters.   **Example:** News at Ten
Write these titles in the same way.

coronation street   alice in wonderland   play for today   ivanhoe
tom and jerry   brixton school for boys   war and peace   the beano

C Write these sentences. Put in capital letters where they are needed.

last week, the film 'doctor in disgrace' was showing at the roxy in sunderland. jane dawson and i went to see it on friday. during the interval, jane had an orange drink called sunburst. she tipped most of the drink over my skirt and i had to have it cleaned at the kraft kleaners shop in newcastle street.

Write all the proper nouns you can find in these notices.

Hornby's sale on today

LOW BRIDGE 13'

Get your DAILY MIRROR HERE

KESWICK via KENDAL →

Personal titles

The first letters of people's names and of titles that go with them must be capitals.

Uncle Sid   **Nurse Lee**

If a title does not refer to a particular person, but is used generally, it has a small letter.

Examples:
Have any of your **u**ncles been abroad?

The main hall was full of **n**urses.

A Write these sentences. Put in capital letters where they are needed.

1 on thursday, helen jones went off on holiday to majorca.

2 mr and mrs carter are related to doctor charles lamperton.

3 professor marion busby is staying with lord and lady brown this week.

B Write these sentences. Put in capital letters where they are needed.

1 the fifty policemen and policewomen outside the hall were under the command of chief inspector smith.

2 Of all nelson's captains, admiral collingwood was the greatest.

3 mrs white said that the church was full of amanda's uncles and aunts.

4 bishop newton asked all the rectors, vicars and deans to wear their robes.

Write the names of these people correctly and change the order of the letters on their cards to find out what they do for a living.

Example:

fan more	foreman	sit dent	fir name	the care	most pan
mr j. moss	Mr J. Moss	miss doe	mr lane	mrs ray	mr myatt

Dictionary order by second letters

Words in a dictionary are arranged in alphabetical order.

All words beginning with **a** come first. They are arranged in the alphabetical order of their second letters.

Example: able   acorn   adore   after   again

A Write the word from each set that would come first in a dictionary.

1 beg   bar   but   4 axe   away   arch   7 grit   gear   gone
2 car   coin   cinder   5 shop   stop   seal   8 lead   link   lamb
3 then   trim   turn   6 oven   omen   open   9 pylon   port   pray

B Write each of these sets of words in alphabetical order.

1 among   any   ajar   always   apt   4 ebb   eager   eclair   edit   eel
2 atlas   art   avenue   asleep   aunt   5 trip   this   team   tank   twist
3 bed   bath   box   bin   bus   6 tent   tube   today   time   tax

C Here are four jumbled sentences. Make sense of them by writing their words in alphabetical order.

1 collects foreign Brian stamps.   3 gave lots boy of A them big him.
2 shown he Has to them you?   4 of keeps upstairs them most He.

Copy these two puzzles on squared paper. Write the words printed beside each puzzle into the squares in alphabetical order. The green panels will give you the name of the shapes.

delta
light
elope
brown
fence
cable

n
e
a
e
e
t

sixty
spine
stage
sweet
scare
surly
shock
sneak
seven

17

Pronouns

> A pronoun is a word that stands in place of a noun.
>
> The common pronouns are:
>
> **I you he she it we**
>
> **they me him her us them**
>
> **Example:**
>
> The dog was howling because **it** was locked outside.
>
> The use of the pronoun **it** avoids writing 'dog' twice in one sentence.

A Choose pronouns from the box to replace the green words.

we she it they he

1 My uncle could not get into the shed because my uncle had lost the key.

2 Jean and Emma thought that Jean and Emma had won the three-legged race.

3 Andrew and I held up the flag to signal that Andrew and I were ready.

4 Melanie was sure that Melanie would be chosen to present the flowers.

5 The fox slipped into the wood and kept running until the fox was safe.

B Find and write the ten pronouns in these sentences.

I was out this morning with Peter when we met Lynne. She had a dog with her. Usually, dogs take no notice of me but this one growled and tried to attack us. Do you think that there is something about Peter that makes them dislike him? Lynne said that it is normally a friendly dog.

Copy this puzzle on squared paper. Fill in the missing letters to make four pronouns.

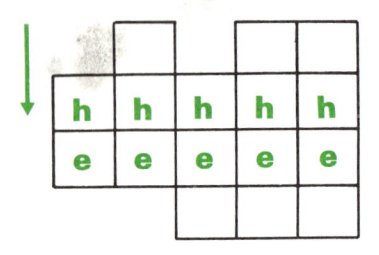

Special pronouns

who, **which** and **that** are special pronouns. They may be used to join sentences together. Usually they refer to nouns that have gone before, but they may stand on their own.

who refers to people.
Example:
This is the man **who** helped me.

which and **that** refer to things and animals.
Example:
This is the car **that** he stole.

A Write the noun to which the pronoun in green refers in each sentence.
1 Is this the elm which is dying?
2 This is the model that I made.
3 The road which he took is blocked.
4 Containers which burn are banned.

B Write these sentences. Use who or which to fill the spaces.
1 That is the man —— sold me the watch —— fell to pieces.
2 The cat —— scratched me belongs to the lady —— lives next door.
3 Is he the guest —— complained about the window —— was shut?

C Join these sentences by replacing the green word with who or which.
1 Mr Green lent me a book. It was all about making kites.
2 My friend showed me the castle. It is supposed to be haunted.
3 I met a girl. She used to live on an island which had no school.

Find the eight pronouns in this passage. Write their last letters in order to make two more pronouns.

That is the house which he bought. They say it is haunted by a ghost which roams the attics looking for Squire Elwood. He is said to have found a burglar hiding in the attic and to have murdered him.

19

Plurals: words ending in ch and sh

Plurals are words meaning more than one.

The plurals of nouns ending in **sh** or **ch** are made by adding **es**.

Examples:
wish → wishes
stitch → stitches
crash → crashes

A Add es to these nouns to make them into plurals.

latch   sash   trench   gash   ditch   catch   punch   rush   batch
march   lunch   dish   winch   coach   wash   radish   rash   finch

B Write words ending in **ches** or **shes** which fit these meanings.

1. homes for pet rabbits
2. sandy places by the sea
3. fruits containing stones
4. places where people worship God
5. large flightless birds from Africa
6. shelters to protect doorways

C Write these sentences. Change the green words into their plurals.

A cold wind was blowing across the marsh. Two tramp sat by the ash of their fire. Both man had patch on their thin coat. There were dry stick under the bush but they could not re-light the charred ember of their fire because they had used all their match.

Write plural words to fit these pictures.

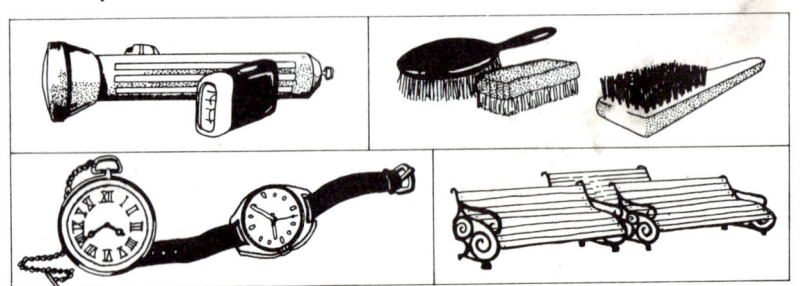

Can you think of three trees with names ending in **ch** or **sh**?

20

Plurals: words ending in ay, ey, oy, uy

Plurals of words ending in **ey, ay, oy** and **uy** are formed by adding **s**.

Example:

holiday → holidays

Remember: Plurals of words ending in a consonant followed by **y** are formed by changing the **y** to **ies**.

Example:

spy → spies   jelly → jellies

A When you have studied the rules carefully, write the plurals of these words.

day alley pony bay locality fly alloy fancy lily

fairy jay motorway filly storey story covey journey

B Write these sentences. Change the green words into their plurals.

1 The first ray of sunlight reached the valley late in the morning.

2 At first light, the castaway swam out to the anchored galley.

3 A line of buoy marked the channel from the sea to the quay.

C y plurals are mixed with ey, ay, oy and uy plurals in these sentences. Write the sentences and change the green words into their plurals.

1 Our family have visited almost all the abbey in Yorkshire.

2 On the trolley were three tray, all piled high with berry.

3 The baby dropped the key down a drain in Mount Street.

Write the plurals of the words ending in y suggested by the pictures.

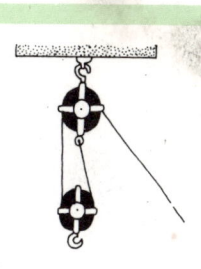

Revision

A Write the plurals of these words.

day   bully   latch   cherry   quarry   dish   ally   bunch   worry
gash   way   witch   brooch   gulch   decoy   gully   batch   bench

B Write these sentences, choosing the correct word from the brackets.

1 I saw the car (who that) crashed.

2 He owns the horse (who that) won.

3 I know (who that) locked the door.

4 The doctor (who that) saw you is ill.

C Write these sets of words in alphabetical order.

1 glue   grit   gone   game   gust

2 hollow   hamlet   hunger   hidden   helped

3 fungus   frosty   flagon   forest   fender

4 slip   swan   stop   shed   spot

5 mast   mule   melt   milk   moor

6 hymn   huge   hand   hilt   hero

D Make three lists from the words in these sentences, headed COMMON NOUNS, PROPER NOUNS and PRONOUNS. You should have five words in each list.

In August, we are going to Devon for a camping holiday. Tom, who lives at Watford, and Simon, one of his cousins, are coming with us. I shall take a camp-bed, some blankets and plenty of warm clothes in case it turns cold.

E Re-write these names and addresses, putting in capital letters where they are needed.

mr william myers,
17, ditchburn rd,
basilchurch,
hampshire.

miss joan key,
patterdale st,
oldborough,
merseyside.

mrs k. hulme,
yewtree farm,
little dean,
norfolk.

22

Just for fun

A Take letters from the end of the first word and the beginning of the second to make the names of famous British football clubs.
Example: stranger sight → st(ranger s)ight → Rangers

fever tonic   satchel search   cold hamlet   supply mouthwashes

launches terminate   dreadful hamburger   brother hamster

parcel ticket   Christmas token   fatstock porter

B Using the pictures as clues, change the first and last letters of these words to make the names of games and sports.

these   sings   tricked   fold

party   gnat   socket   holy

C Find the names of at least twelve girls in this letter square. You may move from one letter to another in any direction and use each letter any number of times to make the names.

D	A	W	N	Y
I	N	E	D	C
L	N	J	R	A
E	E	A	L	O
H	K	T	M	Y

D Re-arrange the letters in the boxes to make the names of outdoor sports. Begin with the green letter.

in nest   boot fall   he carry   by rug   bale slab

23

Adjectives

An adjective describes or tells you more about a noun.

Example:

adjective   noun
a large aeroplane

Some words that are usually nouns may be used as adjectives.

Example:

adjective   noun
curtain material

Some adjectives are formed from nouns.

Examples:

silence → silent

water → watery

A Find the adjective in each of these sets of words. Write the number and the adjective.

1 deep water   2 famous men   3 a new moon   4 eleven days

5 yellow pages   6 a strong rope   7 many people   8 glossy paint

B These phrases contain words that are usually nouns but are used here as adjectives. Write the number and the adjective.

1 the village street   2 elephant hide   3 a flower garden

4 book shelves   5 car repairs   6 steel bars   7 table manners

8 a window frame   9 the hour hand   10 chair covers

11 a dog bowl

C Write the adjectives that are formed from these nouns.
Example: dirt → dirty

anger   depth   fun   rot   distance   safety   gloom   silk   taste   bravery

Write a sentence containing two or more adjectives to describe each face.

Possessive adjectives

Possessive adjectives tell us to whom or to what their nouns belong.

They are placed next to their nouns: **my, our, his, his, her, their, its**

Example: I lost **my** bracelet.

A Find the adjective in each of these pairs of words. Write the number and the adjective.

1 sweet voices   2 my umbrella   3 ripe walnuts   4 its nest
5 their house   6 grey skies   7 deep water   8 her hat
9 our return   10 twelve days   11 your turn   12 new day

B Write these sentences. Replace the green words with one of the possessive adjectives from the black box.

| his   their   its   her |

1 John and Mike went to the zoo with John's and Mike's uncle.
2 Tim bought Tim's skateboard from a shop in Basildon.
3 The puppy was busy chasing the puppy's tail.
4 Diane said that she had left Diane's purse on the bus.

C Write these sentences. Fill the spaces with adjectives of your own.

Paul had a ―― watch for ―― birthday. The case is made of ―― steel and the face is coloured ――. It has a ―― leather strap and the numbers are picked out with ―― paint.

Find the possessive adjective hidden in each of these words.

honourable   pitshaft   gathered   chisel   rabbits   enemy

25

Verbs: tense

Verbs tell you about either the past, the present or the future. This is called the tense of the verb.

The present tense may be formed in two ways.

1　I live here. I do live here.

2　I am living here.

The second form (I am living here) is called the present continuous tense.

A　Write these sentences. Pick the present tense of each verb from the brackets.

1　Jane (dives   dived) into the pool.

2　This is where he (is living   lived).

3　Dante (will win   wins) the Derby!

4　The curtains (hang   hung) beautifully.

B　Write this story, changing all the verbs to past tense.

Donna works in the Bank. She arrives at work just before nine o'clock. Standing outside the door is the manager with a man she does not know. When the manager opens the door, the strange man follows him in. As soon as they are inside, the stranger pulls a gun out of his pocket. Donna runs out of the door and calls for help. The strange man drops his gun and runs away.

Write a sentence about each of these pictures. Include the verb which is below.

is flying 　　　are building 　　　am painting 　　　are waiting

Present continuous tense

The present continuous tense tells you about an action that is still going on.

It is made by writing an auxiliary (helper) verb with a present participle. The present participle is formed by adding **ing** to the present tense.

auxiliary verb	present participle
is	going
are	dreaming
am	hoping

A Write the numbers of these sentences. By each number write the two words that make up the verb in the present continuous tense.

1. The dog is biting my finger.
2. Swallows are building nests.
3. The leaves are starting to fall.
4. Sit here while you are waiting.
5. I am knitting a winter jumper.
6. He is coming on the next train.

B Write the subjects and verbs of these sentences.

Example:

The wild geese are flying north again.

subject	verb
The wild geese	are flying

1. Torrents of water are pouring from the steep hillside.
2. The captain and first mate are staying on board the wreck.
3. Everyone is waiting for Maria to finish her next painting.
4. I am inviting Peter, Mark, Sue and Wendy to my party.

Write a sentence in the present continuous tense to describe what is happening.

Different forms of the past tense

The past tense of many verbs is made by adding **d** or **ed** to the present tense.

Examples:

turn → turned   like → liked

call → called   hope → hoped

Other verbs, called strong verbs, change their middle vowel sounds to make the past tense.

Examples:

win → won   dig → dug

stick → stuck   take → took

A These verbs form their past tenses by adding d or ed to the present. Write their past tenses.

live look pass hiss clean toast remember pick rake owe

paint follow listen wash mark smoke stare stain laugh

B These strong verbs form their past tenses by changing the middle vowel sound. Write their past tenses.

come fall drink give hold run see sit sing know lose

speak stand steal strike wear swim tear blow bite spin

C Write these sentences. Change all the verbs, which are in green, into the past tense.

The aircraft takes off from Liverpool and flies out to sea. It meets strong headwinds and begins to reduce speed. It arrives over Ronaldsway half an hour late. The pilot circles the aircraft twice and ground control tells him that it is not safe to land. Ground control advises the pilot to fly back to Liverpool. He follows their advice and returns to Speke Airport where he lands safely.

There are twelve past tenses in this line. Find as many as you can.

kneworealisedrewounderstoodrankepthrewardedid

Past participles

When you form a past tense with an auxiliary, you complete it with the past participle.

auxiliary verb   past participle
He has sailed.

Most past participles are formed by adding **d** or **ed** to the present tense of the verb.

Example: sail → sailed

The past participles of strong verbs are formed in a different way.

Examples:

blow → blown   do → done

give → given   grow → grown

fall → fallen   draw → drawn

tear → torn   go → gone

A   Write the numbers of these sentences. By each number, write the past participle of the verb in green.

1. Jock had forget his gloves.
2. The kitten has wash its face.
3. We have rake the lawn.
4. This is the letter he has write
5. Pat had eat all the biscuits.
6. I am well know for my stories.

B   Write these sentences, choosing the correct word from the brackets.

1. He has (swam   swum) three lengths.
2. They have (flew   flown) in today.
3. Someone has (broke   broken) a cup.
4. Jean has (taken   took) the day off.

Complete these sentences with auxiliary verbs and past participles.

The spike —— a balloon.

The ship —— under the sea.

The gale —— down a tree.

Subject and verb agreement

A singular subject is always followed by the singular form of the verb.

Example: Anthony likes fish.

A plural subject is always followed by the plural form of the verb.

Example: Sue and I like tea.

Sums of money and names of popular dishes break this rule. They are treated as singulars.

Examples: Egg and chips costs 75p.

15p is the price today.

Collective nouns are always singular.

Example: A box of tomatoes falls off the lorry.

A Write these sentences, choosing the correct verb from the brackets.
1 Tom and Jerry (jump   jumps) off the bus.
2 Two cows (provide   provides) the milk.
3 £100 (buy   buys) this clock.
4 Ham and eggs (is   are) on today's menu.

B Write these sentences, using the singular verb from the brackets.
1 The line of cars (block   blocks) the way.
2 A crowd of children (follow   follows) the Pied Piper.
3 An army of soldiers (march   marches) across the plain.

Change the order of the green letters to make the names of popular dishes and drinks.

- lemon and mile
- bacon and gegs
- fish and pichs
- toast and armadalem
- liver and nisoon
- tea and scubitis
- port and mleon

Punctuation at the end of a sentence

To end a sentence, you have a choice of three punctuation marks:

1 . full stop
2 ? question mark
3 ! exclamation mark

1 An ordinary sentence ends with a full stop.
2 A question ends with a question mark.
3 A sentence containing a threat or a command, or one expressing surprise, ends with an exclamation mark.

Example: How dare you climb on the roof!

A Write the five groups of words below that either express surprise or contain a threat or command. Add an exclamation mark to each one.

I like snow   Don't say you've lost again   What a dreadful mess

Come inside this minute   Gareth has blue eyes and a fair skin

Halt or I shoot   Eleven o'clock and still in bed   I am nine today

B Write the numbers of these sentences. Decide whether each one needs a full stop, a question mark or an exclamation mark. Write it by the number.

1 Ann is staying with her aunt
2 Do you think he will remember
3 How are you feeling today
4 Whatever will he do next
5 Oh, do be quiet
6 This is a very good book
7 Is this a public footpath
8 What a beautiful picture

Write sentences ending in exclamation marks to fit these balloons.

31

Commas

, This is a comma. One of its uses is to mark a short pause inside a sentence.

Example:

Although he had more money than anyone else in the town, Uncle Albert was very mean.

Where several adjectives are used to describe one noun, they should be separated by commas.

Example:

The nasty, mean, spiteful boy threw a stone at him.

A Write these phrases. Use commas where they are needed.

1 clear cool sparkling water
2 dull wet miserable winter days
3 dirty careless untidy work
4 the deep dark gloomy forest
5 a smart well-fitting suit
6 a wretched broken-down cottage

B Write these sentences. Put in a comma to mark the pause in each one.

1 After a night of driving rain the morning dawned clear and bright.
2 In spite of delays on the line the Glasgow train left on time.
3 In a cave on the far side of the mountain there lived a wild boar.
4 From October until March the park gates are closed at four o'clock.
5 If you follow the main road you will see the castle on your left.

C Write the words in this passage which should be followed by commas.

Out of the dismal grey-green swamp there came a huge lumbering monster. Its yellowish leathery skin was smeared with thick oily mud. Pausing only to flick the insects from its tiny pig-like eyes it crashed into the dense undergrowth and disappeared.

Draw a picture of the monster coming out of the swamp.

Apostrophes in short forms

> **'** A comma above the line is called an apostrophe.
>
> One of the uses of the apostrophe is to show where one or more letters have been missed out in short forms of words.
>
> **Examples:** he is → he's   I have → I've
>
> Short forms should only be used in personal letters or when writing words that have been spoken.

A Match the pairs of words in the black box with the short forms shown in the green box. **Example:** 1 we shall → we'll

1 we shall	2 you have	3 I am
4 you are	5 who is	6 it will
7 he had	8 they have	9 he will
10 they will	11 can not	12 I have

he'd	you're	we'll
who's	you've	I'm
he'll	they've	I've
can't	it'll	they'll

B Write these sentences, giving the short forms in full.

1 He said, 'The floodwaters are out and they're higher than I've ever seen them.'

2 If you can't come before Saturday, we'll have to miss the fair.

3 I'm certain that there's no way of telling who's missing.

4 Mark said, 'She'll be very angry if he's not back before dark.'

Learn these short forms and their meanings.

o'clock
of the clock

won't	will not
shan't	shall not

fo'c's'le
forecastle
(front part of a ship)

33

Revision

A Write the numbers of these sentences. Think about the tense of each verb and write past, present or future by the number.

1. They spoke too soon.
2. Lambs are frisking in the fields.
3. John will take him home.
4. Will you ask them to follow on?
5. Mushrooms grew there last year.
6. Rabbits have eaten all the shoots.
7. I shall take the train.
8. We are still cutting the hedges.
9. How old is your grandfather?
10. Angela has forgotten her scarf.

B Here is a table of strong verbs. Copy it and fill in the missing parts.

present	past	past participle
I wake	I woke	I have woken
I choose	———	———
———	———	I have fallen
———	I sang	———
I bite	———	———
———	I blew	———

present	past	past participle
I see	I saw	I have seen
———	I knew	———
———	———	I have swum
———	I threw	———
I hold	———	———
———	I ran	———

C Write these sentences. In place of each ★, put a comma, a full stop, an exclamation mark or a question mark.

Do you like my hair ★ Yesterday ★ I went to the hairdresser ★ She asked me how she should cut it ★ I said that I would like it short ★ What a mess she made of it ★ Once it was cut ★ there was nothing I could do about it ★ Do you think I should go back and complain ★

Just for fun

A Take a group of letters from each of the columns A, B and C. Put them together to make a word. You should make ten words altogether.

A	B	C
ad	vant	age
af	port	fy
en	gu	ope
bun	ter	ow
sup	vel	noon
sat	tro	ment
con	gal	er
ar	gin	naut
as	sid	eer
en	is	er

B Make as many words as you can by putting different vowels into these sets of consonants.

Example: l-d → lid, led, lad

p-t   b-n   h-m   f-r

p-n   t-n   b-t   f-n

C The typewriter used to type these sentences is faulty. It always types an 'x' instead of a vowel. Write the sentences correctly.

Grxy clxxds cxvxr thx sky. Fxnx snxw blxws xn thx wxnd. Wx plxngx xxr hxnds dxxp xntx thx pxckxts xf xxr cxxts. Thx rxbxn pxrchxs xn thx hxlly bxsh wxth xts fxxthxrs pxffxd xxt. Wxntxr xs hxrx xt lxst.

D Write three different letters in place of the ★ to make three words to fit the pictures.

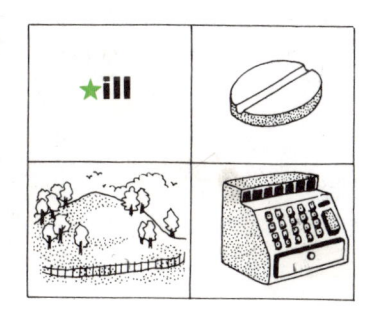

★art

★ill

★ook

35

Paragraphs

A long piece of writing should be divided into paragraphs. Begin each new paragraph about 20mm in from the left-hand margin of a new line.

Paragraphs break up a long piece of writing and make it easy to read.

Each paragraph should contain sentences dealing with a single subject.

Read these paragraphs.

    In 1926, a Great Blue Whale was killed near the coast of Scotland. It was more than 33 metres long. As far as anyone knows, it was the largest animal which has ever lived.

    As well as being very large, whales are very clever. They have big brains and seem to be able to speak to each other in ways that we do not understand.

    Man is the whale's greatest enemy. The whaler fleets hunt them with fast boats and helicopters. If whale hunting is not stopped, these huge animals will soon disappear for ever.

Answer these questions.

1   How many paragraphs are there?

2   How many sentences are there in each paragraph?

3   Give each of the paragraphs one of these titles.

    • Whales Have Big Brains Too! • The Largest Animal Ever Known • The Disappearing Whale

4   Write a paragraph of your own, saying why whales should not be allowed to disappear from the earth.

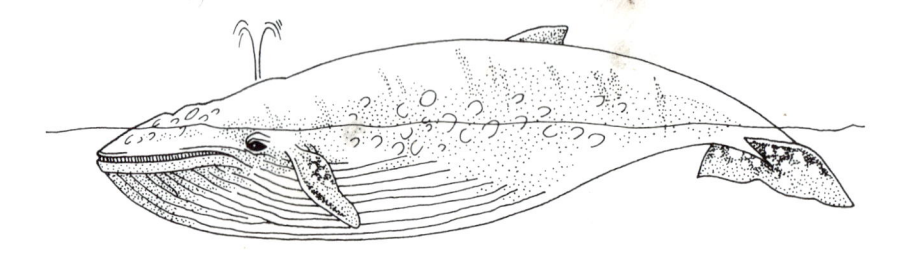

Paragraphs in stories

Dividing a story into paragraphs helps to keep the reader interested.

Each paragraph should contain sentences which go together to tell one part of the story.

Read these sentences.

In a narrow valley beneath Mount Zora, a woodman's hut stood at the edge of a dark wood. Only in high summer did the midday sun warm its moss-grown roof for a few short hours. The hut was the home of Felix Ansbach and his raven-haired wife, Greta. They had a son of eleven years, Hans, and a daughter, Anna, who was two years older. Although the wood provided fuel in plenty, food was always scarce. Felix earned seven marks a week and barley flour was seven marks a bag.

A
1. Divide the story into three paragraphs and write the first sentence of each.
2. Write a title for each of your paragraphs.

B Answer these questions in sentences.
1. How many people lived in the hut?
2. What was Anna's mother's full name?
3. What did Felix do for a living?
4. What fuel did the family burn?
5. Why was the valley dark in winter?
6. How old was Anna Ansbach?

Place these things in order of size. Write the name of the smallest thing first.

| paragraph word letter |
| book sentence chapter |

| second week month |
| day minute hour |

| house town country |
| street room county |

37

Adjectives: countries

Adjectives may be formed from names of countries.

Some end in **ish**.

Examples:

English   Scottish

If the country's name ends in **a**, the adjective is usually made by adding **n**.

Examples:

Russia-n   India-n   Cuba-n

Some change the last letters to end in **an**.

Examples:

Italian   Belgian

A few change completely.

Examples:

Wales → Welsh   Switzerland → Swiss

Greece → Greek   Holland → Dutch

A   Make adjectives from these names of countries.

America   Zambia   Algeria   Rumania   Uganda   Libya   China   Syria
Malaysia   Australia   Nigeria   Ireland   Mexico   Canada   Norway

B   Re-write these phrases using adjectives.
Example: wine from France → French wine

1   sugar from Jamaica
2   currants from Greece
3   wheat from Canada
4   oil from Arabia

5   cheese from Holland
6   dates from Algeria
7   bacon from Denmark
8   carpets from Persia

Change the order of the letters on top of each box to find what it contains.

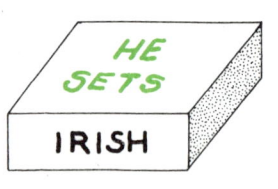

TON COT — INDIAN

HE SETS — IRISH

THE GILD — TURKISH

38

Confusing words: their, there

Some pairs of words, such as **there** and **their**, sound alike but have different meanings and spellings.

'their' always means 'belonging to them'.

In all other cases, write 'there'.

Example: Their house is over **there**.

You may use your dictionary to help with these exercises.

A Write these sentences, choosing the correct word from the brackets.

Last year, Val and Tom (flue   flew) to New York (to   too) visit (their   there) uncle. Uncle Joe said that he (wood   would) be (their   there) to (meet   meat) them at the airport. The (plain   plane) was delayed by (ruff   rough) weather and they had to (wait   weight) for (to   two) hours before they were (allowed   aloud) to land. When they reached the waiting area, (their   there) was (know   no) sign of Uncle Joe! When he finally arrived, an (hour   our) later, he explained that he had (bean   been) at the airport all (mourning   morning) but when they failed (to   too) arrive at the (write   right) time, he had decided that they had (mist   missed) the plane in England.

B Write a word which sounds exactly like each of these.

1 beach 2 blew 3 pair 4 rode 5 here 6 maid 7 seam

Choose the word that fits each picture.

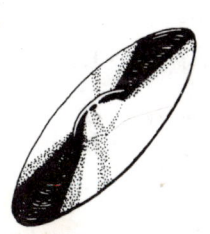

sail   sale   pale   pail   symbol   cymbal   signet   cygnet

Short forms of words

Some well-known words have short forms that everyone uses.

Example: Road → Rd

Put a full stop after a short form if the last letter is missed out.

Terrace → Terr.

If the last letter is part of the short form, no full stop is needed.

Limited → Ltd

Do not put full stops after short forms of metric weights and measures.

gram → g

A Match the short forms in the green box with the full words in the black box.

| Rd Rev. km Wilts. |
| Col Dr Staffs. vol. |
| Sec. Co. Mfg Hon. |
| Cres. Esq. hr Wm |
| Mr Maj. m |

Road   kilometre   Wiltshire   Reverend
Staffordshire   Doctor   volume   Colonel
Company   Manufacturing   Secretary
Honorary   Esquire   hour   William
Mister   Crescent   Major   metre

B Five of these short forms are usually followed by a full stop. Write the five.

Captain Capt   Limited Ltd   Yorkshire Yorks   millilitre ml

Department Dept   Corporal Corp   minute min   Avenue Ave

Write the short forms on these packages in full.

BLIND CORD 20 m

TEA 227 g

METAL TAPE 75 cm

ICING SUGAR 1 kg

DOUBLE CREAM 40 ml

40

Short forms: initials

> The words making up names of awards, titles, companies, etc. are often shortened to their first letters.
>
> **Examples:** Royal Navy → R.N.
> British Rail → B.R.
>
> You may write them either with or without full stops.
>
> **Example:** B.B.C. or B B C
>
> Most school dictionaries contain lists of short forms.

A Match the full names in the black box with their short forms in the green box.

1 Master of Arts 2 New Zealand 3 North	Q.C. N.Z.
4 Distinguished Service Order 5 George Cross	C.O. D.S.O.
6 Greenwich Mean Time 7 Able Seaman	A.B. M.A. N.
8 Queen's Counsel 9 Commanding Officer	G.M.T. G.C.

B Write these sentences in full. You may use your dictionary.
1 Col. Arthur Richardson D S C is the C O of the Second Battery, R A.
2 Albert Timkins B A, the M P for S W Leeds, has been made a Q C.
3 The U N plane should reach Auckland, N Z, at 1300 hrs G M T.
4 H M S Superb sailed from the U K this morning, flying the flag of the C in C.

C Write the full forms of these compass directions.
SW NE E SE NW NNE SSW ESE

Match these short forms with the pictures. Find out their meanings.

STD RAF
MCC

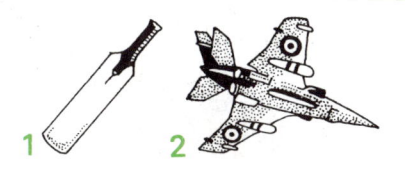

1 2 3

41

Unusual plurals

Some words have plurals that are exactly the same as their singulars.

Examples:

fish   cod   trout   salmon

mackerel   dozen   deer

one sheep

two sheep

Some words are always plural.

Examples:

trousers   pliers

scissors   spectacles

tweezers   thanks

A Write these sentences, choosing the correct plural from the brackets.
1 We caught two (salmon   salmons) today.
2 The (deers   deer) are on the hill.
3 A shoal of (fish   fishes) swam away.
4 (Cod   Cods) are caught regularly.
5 I bought two (dozen   dozens) eggs.
6 The stream is full of (trout   trouts).

B Write these sentences. Put either is or are into each space.
1 These trousers —— worn out.
2 These —— my new spectacles.
3 —— these black pliers yours?
4 This pair of scissors —— blunt.
5 Our thanks —— due to Mr Ben.
6 This salmon —— the biggest.

These are all pairs of things. Draw the joined-together pairs — those with names that are always plurals. Write their names.

42

Plurals: words ending in f and fe

Some words ending in **f** and **fe** form their plurals by changing the **f** or **fe** to **ves**.

The plurals of words ending in **ff** are made by adding **s**.

Learn these lists.

Change f or fe to ves	Both ves and s are correct	Add s
half wolf shelf sheaf	wharf hoof	roof dwarf chief cliff
calf thief scarf elf		handkerchief proof gulf
loaf knife wife life		waif safe reef sheriff

A Write the plurals of these words.

life cliff loaf dwarf reef hoof cuff wolf gulf half wife
calf skiff proof whiff wharf handkerchief bailiff plaintiff

B Write these sentences. Change the green words into their plurals.

The thief climbed across the roof of the adjoining building. They opened the skylight with their knife and helped himself to the content of all the shelf. Their loot included a number of watch and some box of linen handkerchief and silk scarf. Neither of the two safe was touched.

Copy this puzzle on squared paper. Fill in words beginning or ending with f to fit the clues

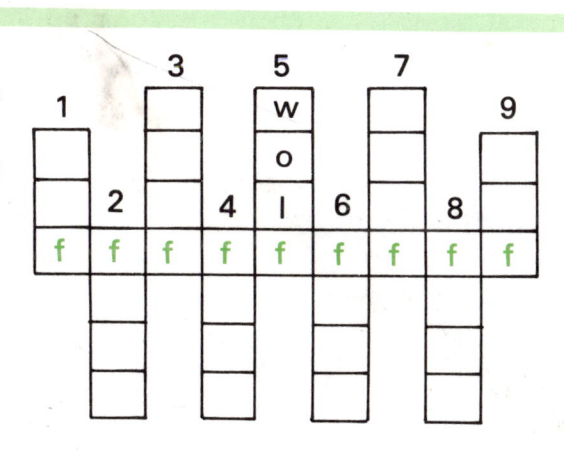

1 small fairy
2 banner
3 young cow
4 rage
5 wild dog
6 tumble
7 bread
8 number
9 opposite of 'on'

43

Three common mistakes

When **I** forms part of the subject of a sentence that includes other people, it should be written last.

Example:

'Kevin, Tim and I all won.'

all right must always be written as two words.

Example:

'Do you think it will be all right for me to come with you?'

If you **win** a race, you will **beat** other people. You must never write, 'I won Kevin and Tim.'

A Write these sentences. Fill the spaces with win, won, beat or beats.

1 John can —— everybody at marbles.

2 You must try to —— this race.

3 Sailor's Song —— the last race.

4 I —— Simon in the 100 metres.

5 Whoever —— Helen will be the champion.

6 Mrs Porter —— £15 at Bingo.

B Write these sentences, choosing the correct phrase from the brackets.

1 (Olwen, Grace and I   Me, Olwen and Grace) went to the fair today.

2 (Me and Carl   Carl and I) took the dogs for a walk across the field.

3 (I and Brian   Brian and I) have entered for the three-legged race.

4 (Me and my sister   My sister and I) go to the baths on Fridays.

How many three-letter words can you find in this puzzle? Read from left to right and from top to bottom. There are at least eight.

			a	l	s	o		
			a	l	w	a	y	s
	a	l	r	e	a	d	y	
			a	n	o	t	h	e	r
	a	l	t	o	g	e	t	h	e	r

44

Names and addresses

You write your own address at the top right-hand side of a letter like this.

28, North Avenue, ← commas
Hove,
East Sussex. ← full stop
BN3 8UA

capital letters

The address on an envelope is written in the same way. All the proper nouns begin with capital letters.

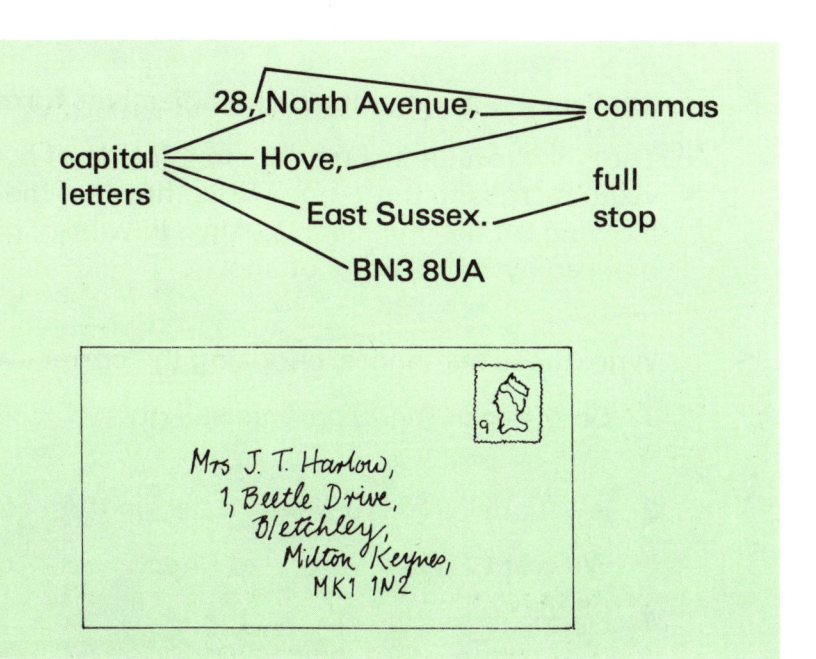

Mrs J. T. Harlow,
1, Beetle Drive,
Bletchley,
Milton Keynes,
MK1 1NZ

A Draw an envelope shape. Write your own name and address on it.

B Write these names and addresses. Put in capital letters, full stops and commas where they are needed.

mr and mrs henry morgan
89 roseville avenue
abingdon
oxfordshire
ox13 6ta

captain parry-thomas
penny lane
westbury-on-trym
bristol
bs9 4dg

Match the short forms you find in addresses in the green box with the full names in the black box.

| St   Rd   Ave   P.O. Box |
| Capt.   c/o   I. of W.   Maj. |

| Isle of Wight   Street   care of   Avenue |
| Captain   Major   Post Office Box   Road |

45

Revision

A Replace the green nouns with adjectives formed from them.

The Italy frontier lies on the shelter side of a height mountain. Soon after visitors cross to the France side, they feel the ice blast of strength winds blowing off the Switzerland Alps. In winter, the twist road is often blocked by depth drifts of snow.

B Write these sentences, choosing the correct word from the brackets.

1 Do (there   their) parents still go (to   too) Leeds every (week   weak)?

2 Is (there   their) a (leak   leek) in the (cellar   seller) wall?

3 We went (there   their) to (hear   here) a (steel   steal) band.

4 Linda (through   threw) the (ball   bawl) straight (to   too) Peter.

5 We (herd   heard) a screech when (their   there) car (breaks   brakes) failed.

C Write the plurals of these words.

half   sheep   sheaf   roof   wolf   dwarf   loaf   deer   calf

salmon   scarf   proof   gulf   thief   trout   shelf   cod   reef

D Write the short forms of these words and names.

kilometre   gram   National Coal Board   Imperial Chemical Industries

centimetre   millimetre   Royal Academy   British Airways   Captain

Limited   Football Association   Independent Broadcasting Authority

E Write this sentence, choosing the correct words or phrases from the brackets.

(Helen and I   Me and Helen) are going to try to (beat   win) Mary and Susan if the lifeguard thinks that it is (alright   all right) for us to go into the sea.

46

Just for fun

A Make as many three-letter words as possible from the letters in these flowers. The middle letter must be in every word.

Example:
f-i-g → fig

B Take letters from the end of the first word and the beginning of the second to make names of fruits.
Example: Linda teaches → Lin(da te)aches → date

chop lumps   sweetpea champion   agile monkey   richer rye

urban anarchy   cheap pleasure   chief igloo   type article

Tudor anger   Capri cottage

C This puzzle is made up of pairs of words, one plural and the other singular. The plurals are numbered and their letters are jumbled. Write their numbers and change the order of the letters to write them correctly.

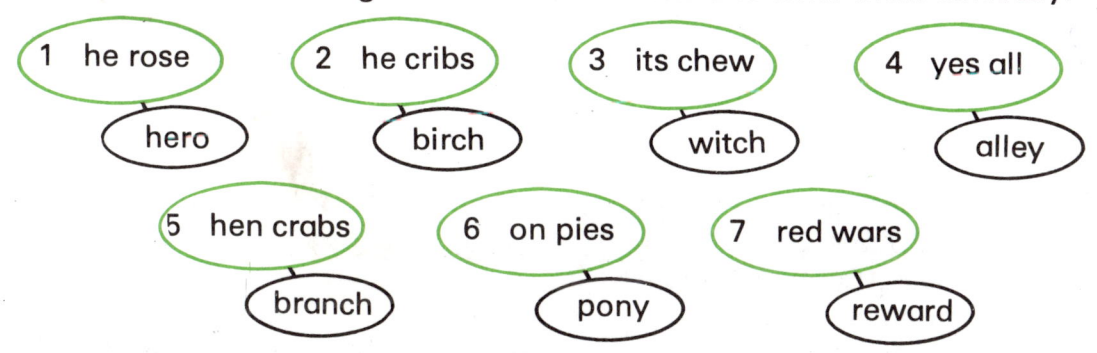

1 he rose — hero
2 he cribs — birch
3 its chew — witch
4 yes all — alley
5 hen crabs — branch
6 on pies — pony
7 red wars — reward

D Change the first letter of each word to make the name of a part of the body.

car   band   beg   read   singer   lose   hoot   rye   pair   dip   peel   thin

sack   south   hoe   half   calm   beck   grist   booth

47

Index

a/an
adjectives
adjectives: countries 38
adjectives: nouns as
 adjectives 24
adjectives: possessive 25
alphabetical order 17
apostrophes in short forms 33
auxiliary verbs 27
capital letters
capital letters: titles 16
commas 32
compound words
consonants
confusing words
confusing words: there/their 39
conjunctions 9
exclamation marks 31
full stops 31
full stops: after short
 forms 40
initials 41
letter writing: names and
 addresses 45
negatives 10
nouns
nouns: common 14, 15
nouns: proper 15
nouns: used as adjectives 24
numbers
object: of a sentence
opposites
paragraphs 36, 37
past participle 29
plural words
plural words: ending **sh, ch** 20

plural words: ending **f, fe** 43
plural words: ending **y** 21
plural words: unusual 42
predicate: of a sentence 6
pronouns 18, 19
present participle 27
punctuation 31, 32, 45
question marks 31
sentences
sentences: compound 8
sentences: simple 6, 7
short forms
short forms: initials 41
short forms: titles 41
short forms: weights and
 measures 40
short forms: with
 apostrophes 33
singular words
subject: of a sentence 6, 7, 30
titles 16, 41
verbs
verbs: agreement with subject 30
verbs: auxiliary 27
verbs: tense 26-29
verbs: strong 28, 29
vowels
words
words: short form 33, 40, 41
words: order 11

The green number shows that you will find information on that subject in *Nelson Grammar Book One*.

48